NO LONGER PROPERTY OF
SEATTLE PUBLIC LIBRARY

Susan B. Anthony
A LIFE OF FAIRNESS

by Jennifer Boothroyd

Lerner Publications Company • Minneapolis

Photo Acknowledgments

The photographs in this book are reproduced with the courtesy of: © Bettmann/CORBIS, cover, pp. 16, 17, 20; © John Kuntz/The Plain Dealer/ZUMA Press, p. 4; © Brown Brothers, pp. 7, 11; Library of Congress, pp. 8 (LC-USZ62-104627), 14 (LC-USZ62-100971), 18 (LC-USZ62-2023), 22 (LC-USZ62-106109), 25 (LC-USZ62-78691), 26 (LC-USZ62-88973 © Sarah J. Eddy); Library of Congress, Rare Book Division, Susan B. Anthony Scrapbooks, pp. 10 (vol. 8, p. 147), 21 (vol. 6 (4b), p. 126); © CORBIS, p. 12; National Archives, p. 19; © North Wind Picture Archives, p. 24, © Jim West, p. 27.

Text copyright © 2006 by Lerner Publications Company

All rights reserved. International copyright secured. No part of this book may be reproduced, stored in a retrieval system, or transmitted in any form or by any means—electronic, mechanical, photocopying, recording, or otherwise—without the prior written permission of Lerner Publishing Group, except for the inclusion of brief quotations in an acknowledged review.

Lerner Publications Company
A division of Lerner Publishing Group
241 First Avenue North
Minneapolis, MN 55401 USA

Website address: www.lernerbooks.com

Words in **bold type** are explained in a glossary on page 31.

Library of Congress Cataloging-in-Publication Data

Boothroyd, Jennifer, 1972–
    Susan B. Anthony : a life of fairness / by Jennifer Boothroyd.
        p.   cm. – (Pull ahead books)
    Includes index.
    ISBN-13: 978-0-8225-3479-2 (lib. bdg. : alk. paper)
    ISBN-10: 0-8225-3479-7 (lib. bdg. : alk. paper)
    1. Anthony, Susan B. (Susan Brownell), 1820–1906–Juvenile literature. 2. Suffragists–United States–Biography–Juvenile literature. 3. Feminists–United States–Biography–Juvenile literature. 4. Women's rights–United States–Juvenile literature. I. Title. II. Series.
HQ1413.A55B66 2006
305.42'092–dc22   2005008295

Manufactured in the United States of America
1 2 3 4 5 6 – JR – 11 10 09 08 07 06

Table of Contents

This woman received a sticker after she voted.

It's Not Fair

Have you seen women wearing this sticker? Many years ago, American women were not allowed to vote. Susan B. Anthony knew this wasn't fair. She worked to change how women were treated.

Susan's father taught his children to be fair. He spoke out against unfair laws.

Daniel Anthony, Susan's father

Boys at this school got more attention than girls.

He learned that Susan's school did not teach the girls everything it taught the boys. He started a school. Boys and girls were equal at this school.

Like this woman, Susan worked as a teacher.

A Needed Change

As an adult, Susan knew women were treated differently than men. Women could only work in a few jobs. Men were paid more than women for their work. Susan knew things needed to change. But what could she do?

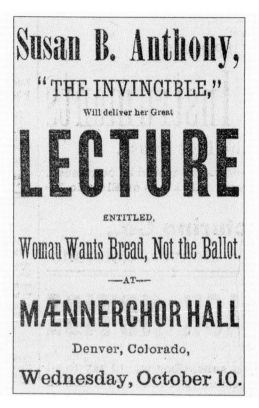

Newspapers announced when Susan would give a speech.

Susan went to meetings and gave speeches about treating people fairly.

Susan met others who felt the same way she did. At one meeting, she met Elizabeth Cady Stanton. They became good friends.

Elizabeth and Susan were friends for the rest of their lives.

Susan was invited to a **rally**. She asked for a turn to speak. The men in charge told her that women should only listen.

Many speeches are given at a rally.

Susan was shocked. Weren't her
words and ideas just as important as
theirs?

These men are voting for president.

The Right to Vote

Susan and Elizabeth knew many laws would have to change to give women the **rights** they deserved. In the United States, people vote to decide the laws. But at that time, only men were allowed to vote. That was it! Women needed the right to vote.

The friends went to work. Elizabeth was a good writer and wrote powerful speeches.

Susan was a good **public speaker.**
She traveled the country to give
Elizabeth's speeches.

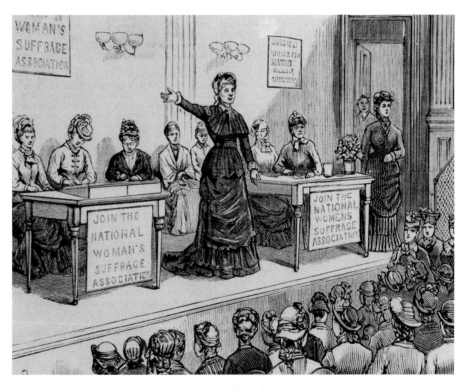

Women spoke at rallies for voting rights.

Their speeches explained why women should have the right to vote. Many people agreed. Most **lawmakers** did not.

A woman speaks to lawmakers.

New-York, December 26, 1865.

Dear Friend:

As the question of Suffrage is now agitating the public mind, it is the hour for Woman to make her demand.

Propositions have already been made on the floor of Congress to so amend the Constitution as to exclude Women form a voice in the Government.* As this would be to turn the wheels of legislation backward, let the Women of the Nation now unitedly protest against such a desecration of the Constitution, and petition for that right which is at the foundation of all Government, the right of representation.

Send your petition, when signed, to your representative in Congress, at your earliest convenience.

Address all communications to

Standard Office, 48 Beekman St., New York.

In behalf of the National W. R. Com.

E. CADY STANTON,
S. B. ANTHONY,
LUCY STONE.

In a letter, Susan asks women to write to lawmakers.

Susan and Elizabeth worked even harder.

To get more people's attention, Susan voted for president. It was against the law for women to vote. Susan was arrested and **fined** $100.

These women try to vote like Susan had done.

THE WOMAN WHO DARED.

Close of the Trial of Susan
B. Anthony.

OPINION AND DECISION OF JUDGE HUNT.

The Fourteenth Amendment Gives No
Right to a Woman to Vote.

MISS ANTHONY'S ACT A VIOLATION OF LAW.

Exhaustive Opinion on the Force and
Scope of the Amendments.

A   VERDICT   OF   GUILTY.

The Champion of Woman's Rights Awaiting
Sentence and Martyrdom.

People all over the country read about
what happened to Susan.

FRANK LESLIE'S ILLUSTRATED NEWSPAPER

No. 1,732.—Vol. LXVII.] NEW YORK—FOR THE WEEK ENDING NOVEMBER 24, 1888. [Price, 10 Cents, $4.00 Yearly.

Women vote in Wyoming.

Never Give Up

Susan continued to give speeches on women's rights until her death in 1906. By that time, the states of Wyoming, Colorado, Idaho, and Utah had given women the right to vote.

Other women continued to work for women's rights.

In 1913, women in New York marched for the right to vote.

All U.S. women gain the right to vote.

In 1920, the government **granted** all women the right to vote. Susan's work was finally done.

Susan B. Anthony believed in **fairness.**
She wanted men and women to have
equal rights.

A woman turns in her vote.

Her work helped give women many of the rights they have today.

SUSAN B. ANTHONY TIMELINE

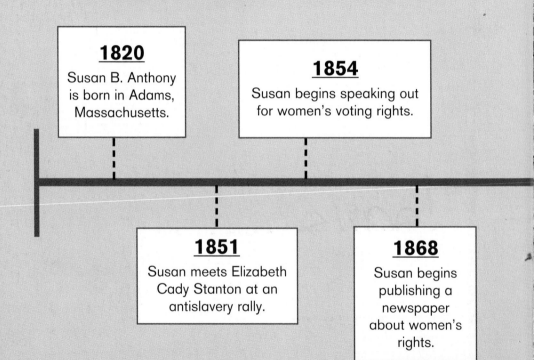

1820
Susan B. Anthony is born in Adams, Massachusetts.

1854
Susan begins speaking out for women's voting rights.

1851
Susan meets Elizabeth Cady Stanton at an antislavery rally.

1868
Susan begins publishing a newspaper about women's rights.

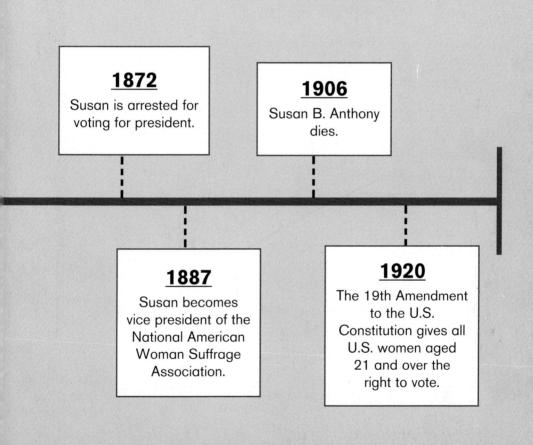

1872
Susan is arrested for voting for president.

1906
Susan B. Anthony dies.

1887
Susan becomes vice president of the National American Woman Suffrage Association.

1920
The 19th Amendment to the U.S. Constitution gives all U.S. women aged 21 and over the right to vote.

More about Susan B. Anthony

● Susan also gave speeches against slavery. Once slavery ended, she worked to give former slaves the same rights as whites.

● Susan made a deal with the University of Rochester in New York. She raised money for the school, so it would let in women students. Susan gave much of her own money.

● The United States created the Susan B. Anthony silver dollar in 1979. The coin is similar in size to a quarter but has 11 edges.

Websites

Library of Congress
http://www.americaslibrary.gov/jb/gilded/jb_gilded_susanb_1.html

Susan B. Anthony House Organization
http://www.susanbanthonyhouse.org

Winning The Vote
http://www.winningthevote.org

Glossary

fairness: treating all people the same

fined: told to pay money for breaking a law

granted: gave or allowed

lawmakers: people who make laws

public speaker: a person who talks to a large group of people

rally: a large meeting held to support a cause

rights: power to do something

Index